The Ultrapreneur

BY **JON ROBERT QUINN**

Introduction

In the ever-evolving landscape of entrepreneurship, where artificial intelligence threatens to overshadow the human touch, one entrepreneur stands as a testament to the power of firsthand experience and intuition. Jon Robert Quinn, an individual who didn't just write about the entrepreneurial journey but lived it, brings forth a unique perspective in a world saturated with books derived from others' words.

As Quinn reflects on the genesis of this book, we are introduced to its roots in a television web-series streaming on IMDB. Quinn, drawing from his personal experiences and lessons as an entrepreneur, recognizes a fundamental shift in the way business is perceived and conducted. Unlike the multitude of business books penned by those who merely regurgitate knowledge gained from reading others' works, Quinn contends that entrepreneurship is an art form—a craft honed through trial, error, and genuine human experiences.

The narrative takes a critical look at the encroaching influence of Artificial Intelligence (AI) on the entrepreneurial realm. While AI, in the form of advanced chatbots like ChatGPT, provides instant access to a wealth of information, Quinn argues that it lacks the essential element of firsthand entrepreneurial wisdom. True understanding, born out of navigating the unpredictable terrain of business, cannot be imparted by a machine that has never built or run a company.

The central question emerges: How can aspiring entrepreneurs navigate the contemporary landscape, where quick searches yield answers but fail to capture the nuance of human intuition? Quinn's answer lies in the pages of this book—a compilation of lessons and insights drawn from the real-life experiences of an entrepreneur who has weathered the storms of business ventures.

The author introduces the concept of an "Ultrapreneur." This term encapsulates an individual who doesn't merely conceive an idea but takes it through the entire journey—from conceptualization to model creation and, ultimately, generating a million dollars in revenue. The Ultrapreneur, according to

Quinn, embodies the fusion of original thought, meticulous design, and effective execution.

This book, born from The Ultrapreneur web-series, becomes a vessel for Quinn's teachings. As the narrative unfolds, readers are invited to delve into the mind of an entrepreneur who doesn't just talk the talk but has walked the walk. Whether you're embarking on your first, second, or fifth business venture, the lessons within these pages promise to be invaluable guides on your path to becoming an Ultrapreneur.

So, let us embark on this journey with Jon Robert Quinn, exploring the artistry of entrepreneurship and uncovering the insights that can truly propel you to excel in the dynamic world of business.

The Money Tree Philosophy:
Nurturing Your Business for Growth

In this chapter, we explore the fascinating concept of the "money tree" – a symbol of prosperity and success in an unexpected place, an auto repair shop. I once had a conversation with a business owner who considered a plant on his desk as his "money tree." Intrigued, he delves into the ancient Chinese myth behind this philosophy and its parallels with the nurturing of a business.

- **The Origins of the Money Tree:** The story begins with the introduction of the money tree concept, highlighting its roots in an ancient

Chinese myth. The belief is that by caring for a plant – watering it, showing love, and providing proper care – one can attract prosperity and financial success.

- **Metaphor for Business Growth:** My client draws parallels between the care of the money tree and the way businesses should be nurtured. The philosophy extends beyond a mere office decoration; it becomes a metaphor for treating a business like a living, breathing entity that requires constant attention and care.

- **Expecting Good Things:** It is imperative to emphasize the importance of expecting positive outcomes in business endeavors. It aligns with the mindset of expecting good things to happen when you invest time, effort, and care into your business, much like nurturing a plant and watching it flourish.

- **Business as a Living Entity:** Business is not just an enterprise; it's a growing, living extension of its owner. Much like a child or a pet, a business demands love, attention, and commitment. I encourage you to view your business as a dynamic entity with its own journey, experiences, and potential for growth.

- **The Emotional Rollercoaster of Business:** Acknowledge the emotional rollercoaster that comes with running a business. From moments of pride and happiness to instances of disappointment and frustration, the journey is compared to the highs and lows of raising a child or caring for a beloved pet.

- **Legacy and Longevity:** A well-nurtured business can outlive its founder, just like a tree can continue to grow and thrive for generations. The analogy extends to the idea that a business can have its "babies," representing new ventures or branches that emerge from the original establishment.

- **Final Thoughts on Starting a Business:** Prospective entrepreneurs are encouraged to approach their ventures with the same dedication and commitment they would give to raising a child or caring for a pet. The mantra is to be present for the business, experiencing the various emotions and challenges that come with the entrepreneurial journey.

This chapter serves as a unique exploration of a business philosophy that blends ancient wisdom with modern entrepreneurial insights, urging readers to embrace the idea of the money tree and apply it to their own ventures for sustained growth and success.

Unlocking Your Worth:
A Lesson from Tony Robbins

In the bustling streets of a small town, Tony Robbins strolled into a convenience store, a place filled with the mundane rhythm of everyday life. Little did he know, this ordinary encounter would become a pivotal lesson on the intricacies of finding and increasing one's value as an entrepreneur.

As Tony entered, he noticed a homeless man sitting near the entrance. The man, looking up with a glimmer of hope in his eyes, asked Tony for a quarter. What transpired next was a simple yet profound illustration of the dynamics of perceived and actual value.

Tony, without hesitation, reached into his pocket and pulled out a stack of hundred-dollar bills. Amidst the folds of wealth, he retrieved a single quarter, handed it to the homeless man, and casually returned the stack to his pocket. The homeless man, now holding the quarter, stared at it in disbelief, shifting his gaze between the coin, Tony, and the pocket that had momentarily cradled a fortune.

In that fleeting moment, Tony shared a timeless truth – "You'll only get out of life what you ask for."

He went on to reflect on the disparity in wealth between individuals like Oprah Winfrey and an average woman bagging groceries. Both had the same 24 hours in a day, yet one was perceived as more valuable to the public. The key, Tony emphasized, lay in understanding and asserting your worth.

In a captivating tale of a business encounter, Tony recounted a conversation with a lady interested in his marketing and coaching services. When asked about his prices, Tony defied conventional wisdom by stating that prices didn't matter. This statement intrigued the lady, who insisted on the importance of affordability.

Tony posed a hypothetical scenario – what if his price were a million dollars? Most people, he noted, would dismiss it as too high. But what if that million-dollar investment guaranteed a billion-dollar return? The point was clear: true value transcends initial price tags.

Entrepreneurs often undervalue themselves, setting prices based on what they would pay rather than recognizing their broader impact on the public. Tony challenged the reader to ponder if they could sell at $11,000 an hour, questioning whether they could deliver $1,000 an hour worth of quality or value.

The essence of money, Tony explained, lies in the exchange of value. As entrepreneurs, individuals trade their services or worth for monetary gain. However, if one is not perceived as valuable to the end-user, they won't receive what they believe they're worth.

Tony introduced a crucial test to determine one's value – the interplay between actual value and perceived value. Actual value is what you're truly worth, while perceived value is how others perceive you. Striking a balance between the two is the key to success.

The story delved into examples from various industries, from real estate to financial planning, highlighting the importance of perception in a world where appearances often open doors. As the narrative unfolded, readers were left with a lingering question – what is your value, and how will you assert it in a world filled with perceptions and realities?

The Three Ps Unveiled

In the realm of successful salesmanship, a triumvirate of principles reigns supreme—Price, Product, and Person. As we embark on this journey, we'll unravel the intricate dance between these three elements, exploring their interconnectedness in diverse sales scenarios.

Section 1: The Foundation - Houses, Cars, and More:

Within the world of commodities such as houses and cars, allure often resides in inherent qualities. Yet, the true architects of successful transactions are the salespeople who skillfully guide the customer's decision-making process. From realtors navigating the housing market to car salespeople steering clients toward their dream vehicles, and insurance agents forging connections, the emphasis lies in the art of selling oneself to facilitate triumph.

Section 2: Breaking Down the Three Ps:

Price: A competitive price is undeniably pivotal, but the sales landscape demands a more comprehensive approach. By delving into scenarios where price alone falls short, we illuminate the necessity of a holistic perspective.

Product: The crux of success lies in offering a product that seamlessly aligns with the customer's needs and desires. Through vivid examples, we showcase the transformative influence a well-suited product wields in steering customers toward the path of acquisition.

Person: Here, we underscore the indispensable role of the salesperson in cultivating positive customer relationships. Anecdotes and examples illustrate how a charismatic and trustworthy salesperson often emerges as the linchpin in closing a deal.

Section 3: Putting It Into Practice - Your Business:

Translating the Three Ps into the reader's business becomes paramount in this section. We encourage reflection on how these principles manifest in specific industries or roles. The discourse extends to strategic positioning, urging readers to be present in the right spaces to effectively sell both themselves and their products.

Section 4: Perceived Value vs. Actual Value:

Navigating the nuanced terrain of perceived and actual value becomes essential. By unraveling this intricate concept, we empower readers to comprehend and balance these values effectively. Aligning perceived value with actual value emerges as a key strategy, fostering trust and satisfaction with discerning customers.

Section 5: The Deal - Phone, Website, or Face-to-Face:

The universality of the Three Ps transcends the medium of sales. Whether over the phone, through a website, via social media, or face-to-face, these principles hold sway. Practical insights are shared to guide readers in adapting the Three Ps to diverse sales channels.

Conclusion:

As we bring this chapter to a close, the resonance of Price, Product, and Person echoes loudly. The key takeaways emphasize their collective importance in the intricate dance of successful salesmanship. We seamlessly transition to the next episode, teasing the tantalizing topic of "Staying in Your Lane." The journey continues, promising deeper insights into the art and science of effective selling.

Staying in Your Lane: Finding Success through Focus

In this discussion, we delve into the concept of "staying in your lane" and how it translates from driving on the highway to navigating the complex roads of entrepreneurship. The analogy draws parallels between staying within the boundaries on the road and maintaining focus within your business ventures.

Defining "Staying in Your Lane"

At its core, staying in your lane in the business world means recognizing your strengths, passions, and expertise and concentrating your efforts there. I want to stress the analogy to driving, where veering off course can lead to problems. Similarly, entrepreneurs can face challenges when they try to do everything at once.

The Pitfalls of Overambition

This section highlights the common pitfall of entrepreneurs having grand ambitions but attempting to juggle multiple ventures simultaneously. The narrative stresses the importance of understanding one's limits and talents. Drawing from personal experience, I emphasizes the need to stay realistic about what one can accomplish effectively.

The Value Exchange

This section explores the relationship between value and success in business. It reinforces the idea that money is the exchange of value for value. Not everything an entrepreneur can do may align with what the market values. Therefore, focusing on areas where one can provide significant value becomes crucial for sustained success.

The 100% Commitment

A key insight is presented regarding the necessity of giving 100% to your business. The analogy extends to the idea of maintaining balance between work and personal life, but also warns against diluting your efforts by spreading too thin across various ventures.

Elon Musk, as an example is involved in various businesses, including Tesla, SpaceX, Neuralink, and The Boring Company, among others. Balancing multiple businesses can be challenging, and it may have both positive and negative effects on his performance.

On the positive side, Musk's diverse ventures allow him to explore and contribute to various industries, fostering innovation and technological advancements. However, managing multiple companies simultaneously can also pose challenges, such as time constraints, potential distraction, and the risk of spreading resources too thin, ending in catastrophe.

Some argue that Musk's ability to focus on multiple projects simultaneously is a strength, allowing for cross-pollination of ideas and innovations across his companies. However, critics have expressed concerns about the strain it might put on his time and attention, potentially impacting the efficiency and effectiveness of each venture, an example would be the falters of Twitter, now known as X.

Lessons from Personal Experience

Explore a journey enriched with personal anecdotes that vividly paint the canvas of a learning curve spanning decades. Unfold the profound realization of the significance of recognizing one's unique genius and skillfully presenting it to captivate the audience. The overarching theme emphasizes the value of authenticity, urging readers to remain steadfast in embracing their strengths and passions. Amidst the dynamic landscape of opportunities, the chapter advocates for staying true to one's core abilities, resisting the temptation of diverging into varied business prospects.

Case Study: Web Design and Email Marketing

An adept web designer for over 25 years, I once embarked on a challenging web design project. The core lesson from this experience revolves around the significance of acknowledging personal limitations. Despite excelling in web design, I demonstrated professionalism and wisdom by refraining from venturing into tasks beyond my expertise, such as building email marketing campaigns when asked to complete the task. This wasn't a service I provided, and knowing my strengths and weaknesses, I respectfully declined.

Key Takeaways:

- **Self-awareness:** The case study emphasizes the importance of self-awareness. Recognizing your strengths and weaknesses is the first step towards making informed decisions in any project.

- **Expertise in Focus:** While Quinn was proficient in web design, he wisely avoided taking on responsibilities that fell outside his expertise. This decision ensured that the project remained within his realm of mastery.

- **Professional Collaboration:** The narrative advocates for hiring professionals for specialized tasks. Quinn's choice to seek expertise in email marketing campaigns showcases the value of collaboration and leveraging the skills of specialists.

In the world of web design, the case study of Jon Robert Quinn serves as a valuable lesson in recognizing and respecting one's limits. By staying focused on his strengths and acknowledging the need for professional collaboration, Quinn not only delivered a successful project but also emphasized the importance of strategic decision-making in the realm of web design.

Time Analysis and Return on Investment (ROI)

- **Time Analysis:**

    - Entrepreneurs are advised to analyze how they invest their time.

    - This involves a detailed examination of the tasks and activities that occupy their schedule.

- **Return on Time Investment (ROI):**

    - The focus is on evaluating the returns generated from the time invested in various endeavors.

    - The term "return" here likely refers to the outcomes, benefits, or achievements derived from the time spent.

- **Significant Return:**
  - If a particular activity or endeavor is not providing a significant return, it may be considered for reassessment.

- **Reevaluation of Importance:**
  - Entrepreneurs are encouraged to reassess the importance of each task or project.
  - If a task is found to be less crucial or impactful, it may be worth reconsidering its priority.

- **Delegation:**
  - Delegating tasks is suggested as a solution.
  - If a task is identified as less critical or not yielding substantial returns,

entrepreneurs are advised to delegate it to others.

- **Freeing Up Time:**
  - The ultimate goal is to free up time for more impactful pursuits.
  - By delegating less significant tasks, entrepreneurs can allocate more time to activities that have a higher potential for positive outcomes.

In summary, this advice encourages entrepreneurs to be strategic with their time management. It involves a continuous process of analyzing the effectiveness of time investment, identifying areas for improvement, and making decisions such as reevaluating, delegating, or prioritizing tasks to enhance overall productivity and impact.

The Ultrapreneur

Conclusion

In wrapping up the chapter, the audience is left with a clear message: success lies in staying in your lane, focusing on what you're good at, and delivering value where it matters most. The journey to success may be challenging, but it becomes more manageable and rewarding when entrepreneurs channel their energy into areas that align with their genius and provide genuine value to the world.

Becoming Who You Surround Yourself With

In the fast-paced journey of life, the dynamics of our social environment often go unnoticed. This chapter delves into the intricate relationships between individuals and their surroundings, shedding light on how our immediate connections can mould our character and guide our path. The central theme revolves around the idea that the people we surround ourselves with serve as mirrors, reflecting back traits, habits, and aspirations that gradually become our own.

Section 1: The Mirror Effect Unveiled

The "Mirror Effect" serves as the cornerstone of this exploration, illustrating the subtle yet powerful influence of our social circles. As we immerse ourselves in the company of those who make excuses for their actions, the contagious nature of their behaviors begins to seep into our own lives. This section emphasizes the inevitability of this phenomenon and its potential to shape our identity over time.

Section 2: Navigating the MLM Landscape

The narrative takes a closer look at specific scenarios, such as the MLM (Multi-Level Marketing) environment. By examining how individuals gravitate towards opportunities present in their immediate surroundings, readers gain a deeper understanding of how social contexts can define professional inclinations. This section serves as a practical illustration of the Mirror Effect in action.

In the vast landscape of entrepreneurial endeavors, Multilevel Marketing (MLM) has carved its niche, drawing in individuals with the promise of financial success and flexibility. However, as the curtains lift on this intricate business model, we find ourselves immersed in a discussion that delves into the mindset of those involved.

The Recruitment Conundrum

A recurring critique centers around the disproportionate emphasis on recruitment rather than the core products or services. Critics argue that some MLM companies, driven by a pyramid-like structure, prioritize expanding their network over the tangible value of what they offer.

Illusions of Prosperity

As aspirants are drawn into the MLM orbit, they are often enticed by promises of rapid and substantial income. This alluring narrative, however, often conceals the challenges and inherent risks that come with navigating the intricate MLM landscape, leaving many disillusioned.

Strained Relationships

Within the MLM realm, participants frequently encounter the delicate task of recruiting friends and family. The pressure to expand one's network can strain personal relationships, raising ethical concerns about the impact of these business practices on the fabric of human connections.

Financial Strain and Inventory Pressures

For many MLM enthusiasts, the journey commences with the acquisition of a starter kit or the obligation to maintain a minimum inventory. This financial commitment can become burdensome, especially if participants struggle to sell the products within their network.

The Positive Thinking Paradox

In the corridors of MLM training, a peculiar emphasis on positive thinking as the sole determinant of success emerges. While a positive mindset undoubtedly plays a role, critics argue that such teachings may downplay the importance of external factors and practical business acumen.

Navigating Misleading Marketing

Aspiring MLM participants often encounter a maze of misleading marketing tactics and testimonials. This creates a challenging landscape where separating reality from illusion becomes an intricate dance, with potential recruits finding it challenging to assess the genuine risks and rewards.

As we explore the multifaceted nature of MLM mindsets, it is essential to recognize the diversity of experiences within this realm. While some individuals undoubtedly find success, due diligence emerges as a critical companion for those contemplating entry into the world of Multilevel Marketing. This chapter invites readers to scrutinize the intricate details, evaluating the business model, compensation structure, and potential pitfalls before stepping onto the MLM stage.

Section 3: The Art of Circles

Choosing one's circle becomes a crucial aspect of intentional living. Whether aspiring to be an entrepreneur, investor, or author, this section stresses the importance of aligning with individuals who personify those roles. The chapter provides insights into the transformative power of surrounding oneself with those who embody the desired qualities, making a compelling case for the strategic selection of social networks.

Section 4: Purposeful Networking

Networking is an essential tool for personal and professional growth, but not all networking events are created equal. Readers learn the significance of attending events frequented by their desired influencers and mentors. The concept of investing time where it matters most becomes a guiding principle for those seeking to elevate their social and professional circles.

Section 5: Stepping into the Arena

To become someone different, individuals must step into the arenas where their role models thrive. This involves not only physical spaces but also engaging in activities and building connections that facilitate access to influential circles. The section underscores the deliberate and proactive nature of personal transformation, emphasizing that success is not a passive outcome but a result of intentional choices.

Section 6: Learning Curve of Growth

While surrounding oneself with achievers is vital, the chapter emphasizes the importance of not being the smartest person in the room. True growth occurs in environments that challenge and inspire. Readers are encouraged to seek relationships that push them beyond their comfort zones, fostering a continuous learning curve on the path to success.

Section 7: Shifting Energy for Success

The chapter wraps up by delving into a personal anecdote, effectively portraying the profound influence that deliberately redirecting one's energy towards aspirational objectives can wield. Through the narrative of forsaking television in favor of immersing oneself in books and writing, Jon Robert Quinn illuminates the palpable consequences of such decisions on the dynamics of conversations and, in the grander scheme, the course of one's life.

Conclusion: The Power Within Social Choices

In summary, this chapter serves as a roadmap for readers to navigate the intricate interplay between personal aspirations and social surroundings. It underscores the agency individuals have in shaping their destinies by deliberately choosing who they surround themselves with. The power to become who one desires lies within the conscious and purposeful choices made in the realm of social connections.

Building a Business for the Long Haul

In the dynamic landscape of entrepreneurship, crafting a successful business requires a comprehensive understanding of the four pillars that form the bedrock of sustained success: Sustainability, Tenacity, Execution, and Positioning (STEP). Let's delve deeper into each pillar to unravel its significance in shaping a thriving business venture.

Sustainability: Navigating the Tides of Change

The Beta Test is Just the Beginning: Sustainability extends beyond reaching the beta testing phase. It's a forward-thinking approach that considers the long-term viability of your product in a constantly evolving market. Entrepreneurs must ask critical questions: Is the product future-proof? Can it adapt to emerging trends and technologies? Building sustainability means creating a model that not only survives but thrives amid industry shifts.

Tenacity: The Grit That Drives Success

Beyond Long Hours: Tenacity is more than just putting in long hours; it's about the ability to endure and persevere through the challenges of entrepreneurship. While many start-ups begin with an initial burst of energy, the key is to assess whether this level of effort is sustainable in the long run. True tenacity involves maintaining enthusiasm, resilience, and the stamina to overcome setbacks throughout the entrepreneurial journey.

Execution: Bridging Vision and Reality

From Idea to Action: Execution is where vision transforms into reality. Having a brilliant idea is only the starting point; success lies in consistent, effective execution. Entrepreneurs must possess the discipline to turn plans into actions. Seeking advice is valuable, but tangible progress comes from taking concrete steps. Regular evaluation and adjustment are imperative to ensure that the business evolves in alignment with its goals.

Positioning: Carving Your Niche in the Market

Unique Selling Proposition (USP): In a crowded marketplace, effective positioning is crucial. Understanding your Unique Selling Proposition (USP) and aligning it with market demands is paramount. Whether introducing groundbreaking products or tapping into nostalgic trends, positioning involves creating a distinct identity that resonates with the target audience. It's about finding where your business fits in the market and leveraging that position strategically.

Reflection and Continuous Evaluation

A Holistic Approach to Business: The STEP framework is not a one-time consideration but a continuous, cyclical process. When faced with challenges or declining sales, revisiting these pillars can provide invaluable insights into areas that may need adjustment. Sustainability, tenacity, execution, and positioning are interlinked aspects that require constant reflection and fine-tuning to ensure that the business remains both relevant and positioned for long-term success.

In Conclusion: Building a Legacy, Not Just a Business

Building a successful business transcends mere profitability; it's about creating a venture that stands the test of time. Grounded in the principles of sustainability, tenacity, execution, and positioning, entrepreneurs can navigate the complexities of the business world with resilience and foresight. Embracing the STEP framework ensures that your business not only survives but thrives, positioning itself for sustained success in the ever-changing landscape of entrepreneurship.

When to Cut Clients

The Quest for Clients

Running a business involves an ongoing pursuit of clients. However, the ideal, lucrative clients are not always easy to come by. Entrepreneurs might find themselves settling for clients who may not perfectly align with their business goals due to the scarcity of big clients.

Staying in Your Lane

The concept of "staying in your lane" emphasizes the importance of focusing on your expertise. While this is generally a good strategy, there are instances where business owners may inadvertently bring on clients who, despite being within their field, turn out to be more trouble than anticipated.

The Short Fuse Approach

The "short fuse" approach involves having a low tolerance for client-related issues. The idea is to quickly identify patterns of problematic behavior and make decisive decisions. If a client seems likely to cause more trouble than they're worth, the business owner may opt to cut ties early on, either by offering a refund or not proceeding with the deal.

Balancing Customer Service and Well-Being

Balancing excellent customer service with the well-being of service providers is indeed a delicate task. Here are some key points to consider:

- **Energy Drain from Challenging Clients:**
  - Dealing with demanding or problematic clients can be emotionally draining. It often requires more time, effort, and emotional energy compared to interactions with satisfied clients.
  - Constantly handling stress and challenges from clients can lead to burnout, affecting the mental and emotional well-being of business owners and employees.

- **Impact on Mental and Emotional Well-being:**

  - Stressful client interactions can take a toll on mental health. Anxiety, frustration, and constant pressure can contribute to a negative work environment.

  - Business owners and employees may find it challenging to maintain a healthy work-life balance when faced with persistent challenges from difficult clients.

- **Consideration for Well-being in Decision-Making:**

  - Business owners often need to weigh the financial benefits of retaining a problematic client against the potential harm to their well-being and that of their team.

- Prioritizing mental and emotional health is becoming increasingly recognized as an important aspect of overall business success.

- **Establishing Boundaries:**

  - Setting clear boundaries with clients is crucial. This includes defining acceptable behavior, communication channels, and response times.

  - Establishing policies that protect the well-being of service providers can contribute to a healthier working relationship.

- **Selective Clientele:**

  - Some businesses may choose to be selective in acquiring clients, aiming for those who align with their values and are more likely to foster positive and collaborative relationships.

- This approach can contribute to a more sustainable and enjoyable work environment.

- **Support Systems:**
  - Providing support systems within the workplace, such as employee assistance programs or counseling services, can help employees cope with stress and challenges.
  - Encouraging open communication and a supportive team culture can also make it easier for individuals to navigate difficult client interactions.

In summary, acknowledging the impact of challenging clients on mental and emotional well-being is an essential step in creating a healthy and sustainable business. Striking a balance between excellent customer service and safeguarding the well-being of service providers is crucial for long-term success.

The Marriage Analogy

Comparing a business transaction to a marriage highlights the mutual commitment between a business owner and a client. The analogy serves as a reminder that, just as clients are hiring the business owner's services, the business owner is also hiring their clients. Assessing compatibility early on is crucial for the success of this business "marriage."

Risk of Negative Reviews

The section emphasizes the potential risks associated with problematic clients, particularly the increased likelihood of negative reviews. Clients who exhibit challenging behavior before the transaction are likely to magnify those difficulties afterward. Negative reviews can harm a business's reputation, making it essential for business owners to identify red flags early and take preventive action.

The Art of Letting Go

Recognizing when a client is not the right fit and gracefully redirecting them to a more suitable alternative is referred to as the "art of letting go." This approach not only preserves the business's integrity but also frees up time and energy to focus on more positive and constructive endeavors.

Conclusion

In conclusion, the chapter underscores that identifying and managing problem clients is a skill that evolves with experience. It encourages business owners to be proactive in recognizing signs, setting boundaries, and making informed decisions. The overarching message is that not every client is worth the trouble, and knowing when to let go is a valuable skill that contributes to the long-term success of a business.

The Everywhere Business

In the intricate maze of entrepreneurship, where success is a journey filled with twists and turns, a pivotal lesson emerges: the heartbeat of a thriving business lies in understanding the difference between being everywhere or nowhere. This chapter unfolds as a valuable lesson, drawing inspiration from global corporate giants like Microsoft, Coca-Cola, McDonald's, and Tesla, who have mastered the art of ubiquity.

Lesson 1: Embracing the Art of Ubiquity

The journey begins with a reflection on the omnipresence of corporate titans, emphasizing the importance of aspiring business owners emulating this strategy. The protagonist, embodying the seasoned entrepreneur or ambitious newcomer, introduces the central dilemma: achieving omnipresence without draining financial resources.

Lesson 2: Strategic Dance with Social Media

The answer lies in a strategic dance with social media. While paid advertising is an option, Jon Robert Quinn advocates for an organic approach. The lesson encourages tapping into personal networks, leveraging the power of referrals, and actively engaging with the community on platforms like TikTok, Instagram, Facebook, and YouTube.

Lesson 3: Unveiling the Power of Traditional Media

As I turned the pages of my entrepreneurial journey, I couldn't help but marvel at the unfolding chapter that revealed the remarkable effectiveness of traditional media. It all began with radio, a dynamic yet cost-conscious medium that seemed to hold the power to captivate hearts and minds.

In the quest for reaching a broader audience, I found myself considering a strategic move — leveraging Other People's Money (OPM) for radio advertising. The allure of this approach was undeniable, promising a reach that extended beyond my immediate resources. However, a subtle caution echoed in my mind, reminding me of the time-sensitive nature of this endeavor. The stakes were high, and every moment counted.

A transition towards podcasts emerged, presenting a dynamic and on-demand medium that offered unparalleled flexibility. Having weighed the pros and cons, found a new path forward, navigating the ever-evolving landscape of media consumption.

The airwaves became my canvas, and the journey through traditional media transformed into a tale of exploration and adaptation. From the vibrant waves of radio to the nuanced and personalized realm of podcasts, each step reflected a strategic dance with the changing tides of communication. Little did I know that this shift would not only redefine my approach to reaching audiences but also open doors to a world of possibilities previously unexplored.

The journey, now interwoven with the frequencies of radio and the digital echoes of podcasts, promised an exciting adventure filled with challenges, triumphs, and the continuous pursuit of innovation.

Lesson 4: Television Spots for Local Businesses

Television advertising has traditionally been seen as a medium dominated by larger corporations with substantial advertising budgets. However, the landscape has evolved, and there are strategic opportunities for smaller enterprises to leverage television spots effectively. Here are some key points to consider:

- **Localized Exposure:**

    - Television spots can offer highly targeted and localized exposure. Local TV channels or programs cater to specific geographic regions, making it an ideal platform for businesses targeting local audiences.

- **Cost-Effective Options:**

    - While national prime-time slots can be expensive, there are cost-effective options available, especially on local channels or during non-peak hours. Smaller businesses can explore these options to reach their target audience without breaking the bank.

- **Tailored Messaging:**

  - Crafting a tailored message is crucial for TV advertising success. Smaller enterprises can focus on conveying a specific and compelling message that resonates with their local audience. This personalized approach can make the advertisement more impactful.

- **Community Engagement:**

  - Television spots can contribute to community engagement. By aligning the content with local events, issues, or interests, businesses can build a stronger connection with the community and enhance brand awareness.

- **Building Credibility:**

  - Being featured on television can enhance the credibility of a smaller enterprise. It adds a level of legitimacy and trust, as TV is often associated with established and reputable businesses.

- **Integration with Digital Marketing:**

  - Television advertising can be integrated with digital marketing efforts for a comprehensive approach. Businesses can use social media, online platforms, and their website to complement the TV campaign, maximizing the overall impact.

- **Measuring Effectiveness:**

  - It's essential to have mechanisms in place to measure the effectiveness of TV advertising. This could include tracking website traffic, monitoring social media engagement during and after the campaign, and conducting surveys to gauge audience response.

- **Consistency in Branding:**

  - Consistency in branding across different channels is crucial. The message conveyed through television spots should align with the overall branding strategy of the business, creating a unified and recognizable image.

In conclusion, television spots, when approached strategically, can provide smaller enterprises with a valuable avenue for cost-effective exposure. By tailoring messages to local audiences and integrating TV advertising with other marketing channels, businesses can leverage the power of television to enhance visibility and connect with their communities.

Lesson 5: Harnessing the Power of Celebrity Endorsements

Celebrity endorsements emerge as a powerful strategy. Every business owner has someone within their network who can become a passionate advocate for their brand—local athletes, politicians, or influential figures.

Lesson 6: Billboards and Other People's Money

While billboards are typically associated with high costs, you're introduced to the intriguing concept of using Other People's Money. This approach opens up possibilities for businesses to leverage billboards without shouldering the entire financial burden.

Lesson 7: Mobile-Centric Strategy

A vital reminder highlights that 80% of online traffic occurs on mobile devices. The lesson underscores the importance of capitalizing on this statistic, urging business owners to place products and brands directly into the pockets of consumers through mobile devices.

Lesson 8: The Ever-Present Strategy

The chapter concludes with a powerful admonition: to be everywhere or risk being nowhere. It emphasizes the need to put businesses where people are and to leverage the mobile-centric landscape for maximum impact.

In essence, readers are left with a profound realization—the journey to success demands not just a strategic plan but a dynamic, ever-present strategy. This chapter serves as a beacon for entrepreneurs, guiding them to navigate the complex terrain of business expansion with wisdom and foresight.

The Art of Resourceful

Marketing

In the bustling world of business, where every opportunity is a potential avenue for growth, I discovered the art of resourceful marketing. Let's dive into a chapter that unveils the journey of turning challenges into triumphs through clever marketing strategies.

Radio Waves of Opportunity

The entrepreneurial journey began with a foray into the world of radio, a medium known for its expansive reach but also notorious for its high costs. However, undeterred by the financial challenges, decided to transform the burden into an opportunity. Wearing the hat of a skilled salesman, I realized that my radio show could serve not just as a personal promotion platform but also as a stage for local businesses to shine.

The key strategy here was to sell guest spots, commercials, and ads on my radio show. This not only helped in financing the radio program but also turned it into a dynamic marketing tool. My philosophy of "value for value" took center stage, as every business showcased on the show reciprocated with added value, creating a symbiotic relationship that proved beneficial for all parties involved.

Billboards: High Visibility, Low Costs

Undeterred by the high costs associated with billboards, I ventured into the realm of outdoor advertising. However, a stroke of brilliance led to a unique approach. The top and bottom sections of the billboard became prime ad spaces, sold to local businesses seeking exposure. The billboard not only promoted the radio show but also became a lucrative revenue stream as businesses paid for the privilege. This clever maneuver turned what could have been a considerable advertising expense into a mutually beneficial collaboration.

Magazine Ads: Doubling Down on Success

The journey continued with magazine ads, where each full-page spread was split between myself and another business. This strategy not only showcased the spirit of collaboration but also doubled the impact and profits. The top half of the ad was sold to another business, while the bottom half became premium real estate for my business endeavours. The profit margins soared, demonstrating the effectiveness of strategic partnerships in the world of marketing.

The Lesson of Reciprocity

Beyond the profit margins and innovative strategies, the heart of this chapter lies in a profound lesson – the power of reciprocity. In navigating the complex dance of commerce, I discovered that to receive, one must give. The intricate dance of value for value became the guiding principle, showcasing that by offering more value to the community, one receives more in return.

Conclusion: The Dance of Business and Community

As this chapter concludes, it leaves us with the resonating echoes of strategic marketing. The entrepreneur's journey is not just about profits; it's a testament to the spirit of turning obstacles into stepping stones. The intricate dance of business and community teaches us that the secret to effective marketing lies not just in promoting oneself but in lifting others along the way. In the grand symphony of commerce, our protagonist chose to be everywhere, intertwining with the community, and in doing so, discovered the true art of resourceful marketing.

Wrap Up

In the culmination of our exploration, the concept of the "money tree" takes root as a symbol of prosperity in the most unexpected of places—an auto repair shop. From a simple plant on a business owner's desk to the ancient Chinese myth behind this philosophy, the narrative unfolds to reveal profound parallels with the nurturing of a thriving business. The essence of resilience and potential within the unlikeliest corners of life becomes a timeless testament.

Transitioning into the realm of successful salesmanship, a triumvirate of principles emerges— Price, Product, and Person. As we embark on this journey, the delicate dance between these three elements is unveiled, showcasing their interconnectedness in diverse sales scenarios.

The analogy of "staying in your lane" transcends the highway, guiding us through the complex roads of entrepreneurship. It draws parallels between maintaining focus within your business ventures and adhering to the boundaries on the road.

The dynamics of our social environment take center stage in the next chapter, shedding light on the intricate relationships between individuals and their surroundings. This exploration emphasizes how our immediate connections serve as mirrors, shaping our character, habits, and aspirations.

A comprehensive understanding of the four pillars—Sustainability, Tenacity, Execution, and Positioning (STEP)—becomes paramount in the dynamic landscape of entrepreneurship. This chapter delves into the significance of each pillar in shaping a thriving business venture.

Entrepreneurs are challenged to pursue ideal clients amid the scarcity of lucrative opportunities. The narrative unfolds as they navigate the intricate maze, sometimes settling for clients who may not perfectly align with their business goals.

In the heartbeat of a thriving business, a pivotal lesson emerges: the difference between being everywhere or nowhere. Drawing inspiration from global corporate giants, this chapter unfolds as a valuable lesson in mastering the art of ubiquity.

The final revelation in the bustling world of business lies in the art of resourceful marketing. The chapter dives into the journey of turning challenges into triumphs through clever marketing strategies, showcasing the resilience and innovation required for sustained success. As the pages of this entrepreneurial odyssey come to a close, the reader is left with a profound understanding of the diverse elements that weave together to create a flourishing business.

Made in the USA
Las Vegas, NV
12 January 2025

16264685R00049